The Stage Costume
SOURCEBOOK

The Stage Costume
SOURCEBOOK

JACK CASSIN-SCOTT

CASSELL

To Rebecca and Tomos, with love

Cassell
Wellington House, 125 Strand
London
WC2R 0BB

First published 1998

British Library Cataloguing-in-Publication Data
A catalogue record for this book is available
from the British Library
ISBN 0-304-35068-0

Distributed in the United States
by Sterling Publishing Co., Inc.
387 Park Avenue South, New York, NY 10016-8810

Designed by Les Dominey
Printed in China through Colorcraft Ltd.

CONTENTS

Introduction

Overture and beginners please! The curtain is about to go up. The audience sits in eager anticipation, but by what criteria will it judge the success or failure of the entertainment, be it a play, musical, ballet, pantomime, opera or revue, that it is about to see?

A stage production is an entity created by the collective effort of individuals. The director, producer, actor, costumier, scenic designer, musician, lighting expert, sound man, not to mention the writer with whom it all began, each contributes his or her individual art and craftsmanship to the joint interpretation of the work to be performed before an audience. That audience is itself an important part of the whole. Without an audience the work cannot come alive.

But without any one of the pieces of the extraordinary jigsaw of different skills that makes up a production, that production will be very much less than complete. The audience may not know, exactly, what is missing, but its enjoyment will be lessened, and the efforts of everybody else involved in no small measure diminished. So when that curtain goes up, success or failure depends as much on the work of the unseen costume designer as it does on everybody else. Of course, the costume designer must not assume it is the costume, rather than the actor, which makes the character a success. The costume is simply the necessary extension of the actor's art, to help him portray that character more effectively.

Nothing evokes the emotions so strongly as live theatre: the look of it, the smell of it, that musty resin aroma that wafts across the footlights into the auditorium. The costume designer has a place at the centre of the whole, exciting experience.

This book shows how the designer sets about creating costumes for the whole range of theatrical productions. It is not intended for designers already fully experienced in professional theatrical design, but attempts to offer ideas and designs to stimulate all those who are interested in the subject. You may find, in the pages that follow, exactly the design you need for your next production; or one of my designs might prompt you to develop it further, or indeed set you off in a different direction altogether. All the designs in the book are there to give you inspiration and spark off fresh ideas.

Research is a necessary part of the designer's work. Gathering historical detail is important, as is careful observation in museums and art galleries, and in everyday life, for although being slavish to the detail of a particular period may be justified, the designer must bear in mind that theatre designs do not usually strive to present literal reality, but are larger than life – their's is an artistic reality. The costumes and settings must appear to be what the designer wants the audience to believe them to be. What he tries to achieve is not what it is, but an illusion. The designer sets the tone, establishes the characters, and brings the audience into the illusion. Theatre arts have proved adaptable to changing styles and fashions, over the years, and for each new production the designer undertakes he meets a new challenge. In revue, for example, and to a lesser extent in musicals, the designer has to use all his imaginative skills to create something different and eyecatching, good enough to hold the attention of a demanding audience. An extreme example might be the dazzling floorshows in the casinos of Las Vegas and Reno, where unlimited fantasy is the order of the day and costumes range all the way from carnival excess to the barest, but most glamorous, minimum. A rare luxury for the costume and stage designer that few budgets would allow, particularly in amateur theatre.

Theatre costumes themselves are as much a part of social history as they are of the study of the visual arts of the stage. The costumes and settings created over the centuries unintentionally mark the passage of time, reflecting each nuance in the ever changing history of theatre. Designers who work in the theatre arts cannot easily be ignored, and their relationship to the sphere in which they work is both subtle and complex.

The variety of costumes needed from one production to another allows the designer freedom to develop and experiment, to move between the bizarre, fanciful and traditional without compromising the intention of the production. All costume and set designing is art accomplished not for its own sake, but ultimately to satisfy an exacting audience. Experiment is vital to the tastes of the present day. What was relevant a few years ago is not necessarily so today. Experiments demand a reaction from an audience.

Theatre art is a subject of much discussion, and whether a given production should be traditional, symbolic or non-representational often leads to controversy. It is as useless to deny the validity of modern art as it is to try to impose it as absolute dogma. No artistic formula can be substantiated or condemned in itself, it must be judged by the members of an audience who are, after all, the main supporters of the theatre.

The illustrations reproduced here capture the overall feel of the productions for which they were created, and stress the continuity of tradition from early times. Each illustration represents a carefully considered subject with a critical and sympathetic appraisal given of the design in question. They will also give the reader a brief outline of how costumes are made and scenic design assembled.

But where to start and where to end? Greek theatre is a convenient starting point as, after all, that is where it all began. But what of the closing point? This is, of course, open ended. The possibilities are endless and will continue to change and adapt with the times. Many of the costumes and sets included in this book could, with a few minor alterations, well serve in other productions. In Shakespeare's plays certain characters, such as Falstaff and Bottom, wear immediately identifiable costumes peculiar to themselves, whilst others in the same drama are in the contemporary dress of the period. Shakespeare's intentions, both in words and design, need to be expressed in terms that a modern audience can understand, whether in traditional or modernistic style. Shakespearean plays are, therefore, interchangeable.

Each production of the diverse plays illustrated, from the works of Shakespeare, through musical comedy, ballet, opera and revue to Christmas plays, has its own costume and set characteristics and, whether performed by professionals or amateurs, demands equal dedication and effort. Every production creates its own challenge and opportunities; some might be experimental, others more traditional. The designer is, in fact, an inventor and should be prepared to experiment with new ways of depicting stage sets and expressing personality and character through costume design. However, available finance must always be taken into account and a strict budget allocated for all aspects of the production. For simple budgetary reasons, true historical accuracy must sometime be discarded, along with elegant, detailed drawing and and the skilled worker to make up the costumes or build the sets. The resulting compromise must then be carefully managed.

Studying costume and set design means not only looking at them but also understanding them. How is a set or costume really constructed? What feature or features are most important? Practice and know-how serve to answer these questions. Forming the foundations is vital so that when viewed as a whole the individual features of the design come to life.

The interpretation of a designer's sketch can be difficult and is often a delicate process; it can sometimes be a minefield even in professional workshops. The examples given in this book are prepared in such a way that they should leave the workroom in no doubt as to the designer's intention. Giving the director the general idea of a design is not enough. It is essential to give as much information as possible to the people in the workrooms, who will ultimately produce the final costumes and sets. A finished, detailed drawing is highly desirable. It can then be pinned up in the workroom for constant reference.

All designing requires some knowledge of sketching, although, strictly speaking, this is not absolutely essential for costume designing, provided the designer has a good knowledge of pattern making and cutting. The most important thing is to keep everything as simple as possible. However, the ability to sketch makes it easier to see the relationships between different shapes. Preliminary sketches in light pencil determine the correct proportions and from these seemingly lifeless geometric lines comes a shape which the designer visualises as that of the character or set required. The designing process begins directly after the play reading. Watching early rehearsals, the designer prepares a breakdown of each character and makes copious notes as each movement, stance or speech may suggest a feature, style or, indeed, a particular colour scheme. The main function of costume design is to provide vital information, such as a character's personal and social standing and the period in which the scene is set.

The designer has a considerable freedom in how he achieves his purpose. Given that the theatre is an act of make-believe between actor and audience, the designer may employ exaggeration to strengthen the illusion, or add to it, but there must always be the required instant recognition by the audience; and the designs must have proper significance to the dramatic enhancement of the play.

Before the final designs are complete or accepted, there is invariably a great deal of give and take between director, designer and performers. Sometimes a rough shape will need to be devised as while transcribing a two-dimensional shape on paper to a three-dimensional shape on a body, unforeseen problems can arise. It is, however, essential that the final costume is as close to the original idea as is possible as unless that is adhered to, the original concept may be lost. Having said that, to dismiss out of hand a suggestion or request passed on by a performer could perhaps be a fatal mistake. The performers must live, breathe, and move within the concepts of the design, so must feel comfortable and, above all, confident wearing it. It would be a cardinal sin to make a performer a mere puppet at the expense of the costumier, scenic designer, musician or lighting expert, each vying to outdo the other in their interpretation of some dramatic expression. The temptation to do so may be great, but it must be resisted.

Designing stage costumes concentrates, for most purposes, on the exterior appearance of the character, the fashion silhouette being an important feature from which to identify past eras. A knowledge of the underwear of the period is therefore very helpful, as often without the correct solid body beneath, the ultimate shape is impossible to realise.

What are the principles that motivate a design? As a costume is a symbol of an epoch, the suitable fabric, cut and colour are the primary objectives of the costume designer. Periods such as the Renaissance emphasised and exaggerated the male characteristics. The female figure naturally enough followed the more seductive principle, the object being to attract the opposite sex by exploiting their feminine charms. Basically all costume should meet three requirements: social – representing the character's position in society; seductive – appealing to the opposite sex; and utility – practical, to give easy movement and comfort to the wearer.

For those wishing to learn the complicated technical aspects of scenery mechanism, which I have touched on only very briefly, or to pursue further research into individual aspects of this very wide subject of theatre, a selected bibliography is included at the end of the book. But whatever your level of interest, and whatever your role in theatre design, amateur or professional, you can be sure there will always be performers to provide the magic that the public want. That magic is yours to share; your designs are an essential part of that magic.

Period Costumes

GREEK ACTOR

Theatre as we know it today in the West originated in Greece more than 2,000 years ago. Even then, costumed actors were performing sophisticated dramas before an audience in an auditorium.

This design shows a Greek actor and his masks. To increase the height of the mask, the top or hair was placed high. A long flowing robe was amply padded to give fullness to the figure, in addition to complete freedom of movement. The masks were made to represent different characters; using masks enabled an actor to play two or three roles, as the law permitted no more than three actors to perform in one play. The construction of the masks was such that the aperture of the open mouth was shaped like a small megaphone. This helped the actor to project his voice to an audience seated

some distance from the stage. The audience was able to recognise each character from the mask being worn, masks being large enough to help them identify the various characters even from a distance. Masks are used in today's theatre in exactly the same way; in conjunction with modern dress, they allow one actor to change character in the simplest way, or can represent whatever symbolic meaning may be required.

Greek Costume

The wealth of information available on Greek attire is very helpful to the costume designer. The outer garment could be in a variety of shapes but always seemed to be studiously pleated. The principal garment worn by both men and women was the *tunica*. The design of the tunic for the woman in this illustration is quite loose, but drawn tight around the waist, over the girdle and concealing it completely beneath its folds. The tunic was adorned around the edges with rich scrolls. The costume illustrated here shows a further external garment covering the upper half of the body, rather like a large bib, being a square piece of material folded double, worn with the border towards the girdle. It hung in such a way that the centre came under the left arm, the two ends hanging down under the right arm. The complete piece was secured by two clasps which fastened the front and back over each shoulder. The hair was built up with a tiara and with numerous gee-gaws. Simple soles with thongs or string for fastening usually acted as shoes.

The design for the Greek soldier is based on research of statues and vases. The defensive armour consisted of a helmet, breast plate, greaves and shield. The helmet is of the immovable type, which had to be pushed back leaving a space between its crown and the head of the wearer. A horse hair crest rose from the top of the helmet. The body was guarded by a breast plate made of a number of small linked slips (pieces of metal). The shoulders were protected by separate pieces, these being fastened at the chest by a cord. The legs were guarded by high over-the-knee greaves fastened at the back by straps. Feet were bare. The usual shield was very large and circular with a broad flat rim and a raised centre. The chief offensive weapons were the sword and spear. The tunic beneath the armour fell only to thigh length.

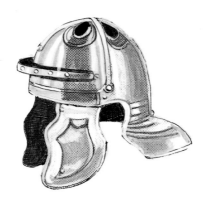

GREEK AND ROMAN ARMOUR

Headwear, armour and breast plates are shown here, suitable for Greek and Roman period plays. Top left on the facing page is an early Greek helmet which enclosed the head completely, leaving a small opening for the eyes. From the centre top emerged a tall horse hair crest holder, giving greater height to the wearer. The helmet top right is also Greek. This one enclosed the head, face and sides, but left the front of the face unprotected. The horse hair crest was lower, but allowed better protection for the head. In the centre is the body armour of a Roman soldier or legionary. Known as *lorica segmentata* it is made of steel strips, fastened inside by leather straps, and closed over the body by buckles, pins and leather thongs. The two helmets on this page were worn by Roman legionaries in the first and second centuries AD. Most stage costume designs follow these patterns.

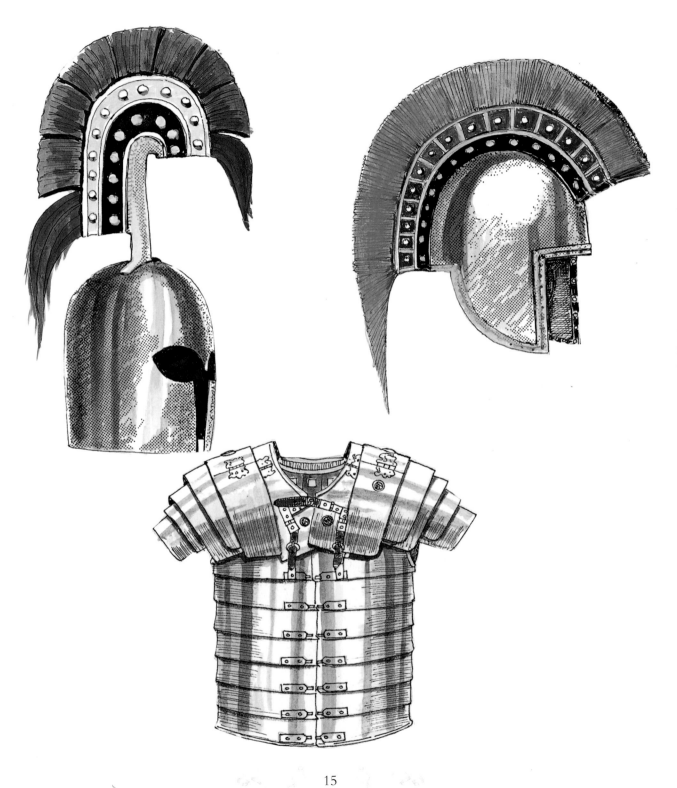

CLEOPATRA

This design is perhaps the easiest of all costumes to make. The tunic style is simple in construction. The origin was probably a length of fabric, long enough to reach the breast line and wide enough to wrap around the figure, leaving a piece to tuck in at the top to keep it closed. The costume shown here is a linen tube, put on by stepping into it and pulling it up, the shoulder straps to be adjusted (see sketch of pattern). The decorated collar part can be made by cutting a circular shape from felt or buckram, and glueing beads on. The headdress can be in felt or papier mache. The middle sketch is taken from the Egyptian tombs, showing all the details required for the design.

EGYPTIAN COSTUME

The designs shown here are from researches of wall paintings, reliefs and papyri as well as evidence given by archaeologists of the costumes of that time. The basic materials were wool and flax, which was woven into linen. Both these designs show examples of the simple kilt or shendyt. The black and white drawing from the tomb is from the Old Kingdom and shows an official wearing a kilt with a pleated overlap. The design on the left is a slightly larger version, which ends just below the knee, so that the lower hem projects slightly forward. These kilts were pleated and untailored, ending with a straight edge and secured by tucking them into the waistband. The design on the right is that of royalty. The kilt reached only to the thighs, tailored so that it gave a three part effect from the front. It was held up by a belt. The headwear represents the white crown of Upper Egypt.

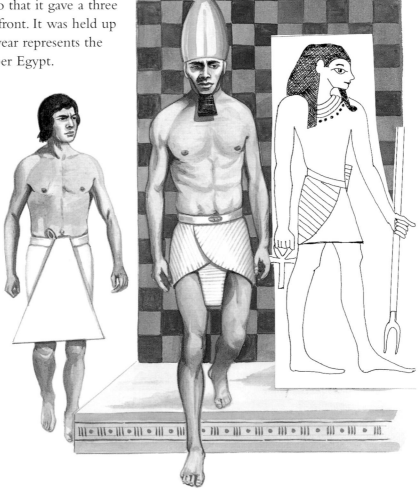

NORMAN NOBLEMAN

The design is set against the domestic architecture of the low round arch and supporting columns of the period. The stone interiors give a cold effect, which can be relieved by murals or bright wall hangings. Wooden benches and long tables are heavy but simple. The design of a Romanesque tunic of the upper classes shows the Norman nobleman in everyday attire. Undertunics were high to the neck, with a slit to allow the head to pass through. The undertunic was long, generally of white linen, with long tight sleeves.

The outer garment, the dalmatica or bliaut, was a neat, close-fitting garment which was flared from the waist to the ground. The sleeves were wider and shorter than the alb or undertunic. The cuffs were emphasized by being very wide and lavishly decorated.

The fashionable nobleman, as shown in the design, had the outer garment draped across his abdomen and bunched up at the hips. To achieve this effect the outer garment is made a little fuller so that, when pulled up rather tightly across the abdomen, the surplus folds into a large box pleat at the back. A cord is tied tightly around the waist, allowing the material to blouse over, front and back. The sketches show the sleeve pattern and the back lacing of the outer tunic. Shoes with pointed toes were popular. The man's hair could be either long or short, and he often sported a beard and drooping moustache.

JOAN OF ARC

The 'Maid of Orleans' is best designed in the costumes of her own period. Apart from the simple white gown that she wears in prison and at her trial, the suit of armour is also designed in white. Joan of Arc has to be portrayed as a saintly young woman, who is outspoken and courageous. Her costumes must emphasize her youth and her courage: she went to her death when she was only nineteen. The armoured costume is best hired from any good theatrical supplier. The page should be dressed in a blue and white costume, the colours of Joan of Arc.

HENRY VIII

This easily recognisable figure, giving an artificial burliness to Henry VIII, shows the heavy square-cut costume of the 'horizontalism' period, which followed the style of the architecture and became the male fashion of the day. This design creates the idea of both set design and costume. The square-style revolutionary English Tudor architecture sets the scene of the period. The design, taken from historical research, shows the costume to perfection. The small-brimmed, wide-crowned cap, worn at an angle, is ornamented with a jewelled design and curled ostrich feather tips. This could be worn both in and outdoors. The short sleeveless gown in a rich, heavy material was voluminous and had large wide sleeves. The side sketches give an indication of the fullness of the long-lapelled gown, puffing out at the shoulders to just above the elbow. The shirt has the fashionable neckline and long full sleeves gathered into ruffles at the wrist. The doublet is worn over the shirt and features large sleeves protruding through the gown's short sleeves, revealing the shirt through the slashed openings gathered at the elbows and forearms. The jerkin was worn over the doublet, open to the waist at the front, with skirts reaching the knees. A leather belt supported a dagger. The coloured hose or stocking were shaped to the legs. The footwear was of exaggerated low-cut 'bear paw' shoes, without heels and very square-toed, decorated with slashings. The legs should appear heavy, even slightly grotesque. This can be achieved by the use of latex (rubber) forming. The body must in most cases be heavily padded and specially constructed with high shoulder pieces to give the visual effect of shortening the performer's neckline.

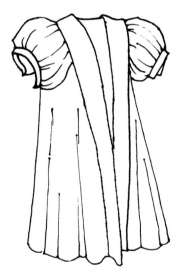

A GENTLEMAN OF THE 1750S

This is a standard design for many plays of the period, and quite often some of Shakespeare's plays have been costumed in this style. The suit consists of a coat, waistcoat and breeches, which remained in fashion throughout the century. The close-fitting coat, waisted and full skirted, reaches to below the knees. The skirt has three vents to hip level. The neckline is collarless. The coat falls in a straight line down the front. Buttons and button holes extend from neck to hem. The flapped pockets at hip level are horizontal and fastened with buttons. The sleeves are loose fitting with a very deep cuff spreading upwards, the wings curved around the back of the elbow, and decorative buttons placed above the bend. The waistcoat resembles the coat in cut, but is closer fitting to the waist. The skirts end at the thighs.

The knee breeches narrow to just below the knees. Gartered stockings are pulled up over the breeches. A cravat, a strip of lawn or muslin, is worn. The shoes have square block toes and square tongues, very high. A three cornered hat is a usual feature. The wigs, in many styles, always sport masses of curls.

LADY HAMILTON AND NELSON

When designing for a play including real personalities, it is important to research as much as possible. There is abundant information about the two main characters in this play. There are also numerous fashion notes regarding what Lady Hamilton wore. The choice depends purely on the budget available for the production. In this case, the budget was modest, so the design fell on the simple styled Regency gown. This classical bodice and skirt in muslin or satin has a low, round-necked decolletage, short sleeves with a high Empire line coming to just under the breast. The charm of this fashion depended very much upon the physique of the wearer. The enveloping silk scarves have coloured borders and brocaded ends. The small headchief contains the classical bunch of curls at the top.

Shakespeare and Dickens

DESIGNING FOR SHAKESPEARE

MACBETH

This Shakespeare play is particularly suitable to be played in its own period. The design shows first the three weird witches bending over their cauldron, floating through the misty Scottish moorland. Long voluminous cloak-like garments, ragged and torn, seem the most suitable dress for them. Make up should be greenish grey with heavy eye make up to produce a bright staring effect. Long untidy wigs from black to grey to red could be worn. Lady Macbeth's dress in the first entrance is designed in the style of a great lady of her time. The pale blue dress is open down the front in a V-shape with a laced-up under-garment. The long sleeves have shoulder pieces. A heavy ornamental belt is also worn. The hair should be long to below the hips and crowned with an ornamental head covering. Another costume, not illustrated, is that of a nightgown for the sleep-walking sequence.

Macbeth himself is wearing a basic costume of a tough Scottish lord, including full hose or trews, cross-gartered from knee to ankle. The fairly loose-fitting tunic is thigh length with the long sleeves rolled up to reveal the arms. A leather belt circles the waist. The ground-length cloak is fur-lined, slit at the sides for the arms to protrude. This design can be worn throughout the play with minor attachments such as swords and helmets. The dull earth colours best express his character.

JULIUS CAESAR AND CALPURNIA

The design captures two figures, those of Caesar and his wife, Calpurnia. The information comes from many sources, principally from museums where many large statues show the wearing of the toga. The main feature of the Roman toga is its size. The length is three times the height of the wearer and the width twice his height. The method of dressing is by folding it lengthways about the middle in broad folds. It is then placed or hung over the left shoulder, leaving about one third in length hanging in front. The remainder is passed diagonally across the back, under the right arm and thrown back over the left shoulder. Because of its width it covers the left arm. The part crossing the back is spread out to cover the right shoulder blade. The corner hanging over the left shoulder is shortened by drawing the toga up at the chest and letting it fall over the folds. These folds can serve as pockets. The toga can be sewn into the desired position. Calpurnia is dressed in a similar way. For the opening scene she should be wearing a long nightgown over a full-length tunic.

ANTONY AND CLEOPATRA

The character of Antony in this Shakespeare play is that of a typical Roman general, dressed overall in military garb. Designed to give the correct feel of the period, the brownish-red woollen shirt reaches the thighs, and is worn against the skin. The protective leather body corselet generally follows the contours of the body. Leather straps descend by way of protection, not only on the lower part of the body, but also down the upper arms and over each shoulder. From knee to ankle greaves are worn for protection, with laced boots. A sword is attached to a sling hanging down on the right shoulder. A long red woollen cloak is also worn. The sketched background depicts the Egyptian location (see page 16 for Cleopatra's costume).

OTHELLO

This is perhaps a rather flamboyant design for Othello, the Moor. This was
the intention as at this stage of the play Othello was waging war against
the Turks on the island of Cyprus. A mixture of costume was common
amongst soldiers who travelled from one country to another and the
Eastern style allows Othello easy movement with his flowing libas or very
full pantaloons. The short sleeveless jacket had gold braid trimming. The
undertunic was long sleeved to the wrist and was worn with a brown silk
cummerbund with a white motif. A curved dagger was attached under the
cummerbund by slings, an important prop for Othello's eventual suicide.
The fez was red with a blue tassel and a large feather fastened with a
brooch. The Moorish-style slippers complete the costume.

Desdemona's costume is a design from historical data, mixing the
periods and styles as Shakespeare himself would so often do. The design for
Cassio is that of the basic Elizabethan costume, with armoured breast plate,
tall hat and neck ruff.

A MIDSUMMER NIGHT'S DREAM

The mischievous fairy Puck turns a poor weaver, Bottom, into an ass. He casts a magic spell on Titania, so that when she awakens, she sees and falls in love with this ass who seems beautiful in her eyes. The design depicts the scene – Titania wearing a long silk gown in pale blue, star spangled, clinging close to the body, simple and elegant. The blond hair (a wig) should be hip length and bedecked with flowers. The design for Puck's costume should be simple and rustic. Here I've used light brown tights with a light beige jerkin worn over a shirt. Shoulder wings, a girdle and a circlet of flowers express his position as servant to Oberon, King of the Fairies. The design for Bottom, the weaver, a mortal, should be conveyed by a rustic costume with well-worn white shirt, close-fitting tights, patched at the knees and back. The plain open sleeveless jacket is of green cloth, lined in red, and is also patched. The ass's headmask with soft ears should be well designed and carefully made to fit correctly and be comfortable over the head. The shoes are soft, but unlaced. The script of his play is carried in his hands.

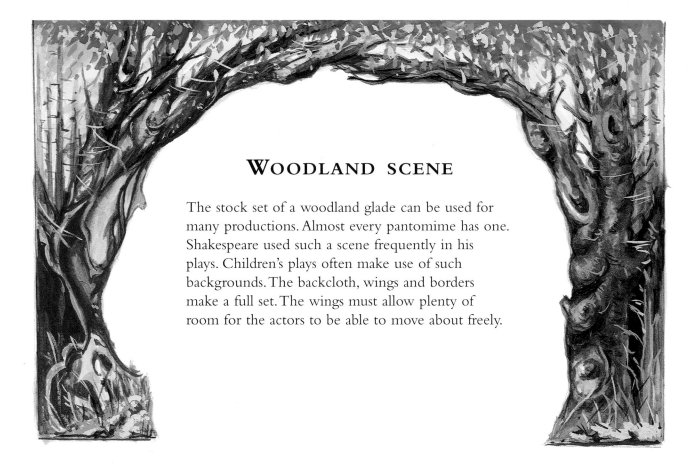

WOODLAND SCENE

The stock set of a woodland glade can be used for many productions. Almost every pantomime has one. Shakespeare used such a scene frequently in his plays. Children's plays often make use of such backgrounds. The backcloth, wings and borders make a full set. The wings must allow plenty of room for the actors to be able to move about freely.

ROMEO AND JULIET

These designs are in the traditional style of costumes of the period, as faithfully reproduced in the works of contemporary painters. Romeo and Juliet were both very young, in their early teens, and both of wealthy families. The designs must both appear youthful and indicate wealth in the costumes of early Renaissance Italy. Romeo's costume is designed after a painting by Vittore Carpaccio, about 1490. Note the square silhouette. Characteristics of the period were gorgeous painted fabrics such as velvet and silk. The doublet had a low neckline with elbow-length sleeves, padded to give the appearance of wideness. The hose were close fitting. The enveloping short cape was slung over the shoulders and fell in folds. The small flat hat fitted closely over the shoulder-length hair.

The design for Juliet follows the fashionable trend. Young women did not cover their hair, but adorned it with strings of pearls or a net. The bodice and skirt of the dress were joined, the neckline square. Two gowns were worn, the overtunic so slit to reveal the beautiful material of the undertunic. Long hair helps foster the illusion of a young girl.

Falstaff and Mistress Ford

Falstaff is a merry, beer-swilling character, universally expected to be fat and jolly in physique as well as temperament. The actor may be that way too, of course, but most likely he will not, so his costume must give the impression of bulk by being padded out. The padding must be made separately to be worn under the costume and great care taken in the making of it. It is a close-fitting garment, in T-shirt style, with the necessary padding gradually built up until the required areas are covered, and only then sewn firmly on to the garment. Once this has been satisfactorily achieved, a larger garment, such as a T-shirt, is placed over the top and sewn on to the undergarment. The actor can then remove it quite freely without disturbing the bulk that the padding represents.

Mistress Ford can be treated in a similar fashion, by padding out mainly the stomach and posterior. The costumes are designed in the manner of Shakespeare's times.

THE TAMING OF THE SHREW

The design devised here represents two locations, the house of Lucento and
the city of Padua. Two insets were built, one beside the other, both idealised
pictures of the epoch. Each scene can be masked by a curtain when not in
use, or by lighting. Lights can reveal only such a part of the stage as is
required, and all else can be in darkness.

PETRUCHIO

Petruchio, a gentleman of Verona, is a flamboyant
character, so must be costumed as such. In both the
play and the musical *Kiss Me Kate* (see page 64) the
costume is important. The challenge of interpreting
this dominant character is manifold. He has
unflagging energy and the humour of an
infectious music-hall type of extravagance. So the
costume needs an air of languid sensuality. The
outline needs to follow the fashionable shape of
the time. The linen or cambric shirt is worn
beneath a sleeved waistcoat. Over this is a
high-necked sleeveless doublet, with the
front padded to a point below the waist.
The long sleeves are made in a different
material from the doublet, usually
detachable. The ties that hold the
sleeves to the doublet are concealed by
small roll wings. The short hose are padded
out and have bands of embroided material
worn with nether stockings and slashed
shoes. A small gathered beret, a copotain,
is worn at an angle.

SOLDIER

This design for a soldier can be used in many plays, including those of Shakespeare, where the minimum of armour is required. A short-sleeved, thigh-length chain armour coat is worn over a long-sleeved undergarment. Attached to the coat is a neck and head protection, also of chain armour, over which is a dish-shaped helmet. Covering the armour is a sleeveless leather jerkin which is also thigh length. From the belt is attached a strap from the left. The legs are covered with short canions and cloth tights in heraldic colours. The feet are covered in leather heel-less open shoes. Behind the figure are the shapes of various halberds, sword and daggers, all used in this type of production.

BATTLE SCENE

This design is for a battle scene in which it is necessary to convey the spirit and period of the event on a very small area of stage. The stage itself must be kept relatively clear to leave plenty of room for the actors. Shakespeare's plays are well known for their energetic fight scenes. The symbolic tents create the correct atmosphere. The lighting should convey the impression of a pending bloodshed.

RENAISSANCE COSTUME

This design follows the Italian fashion of the Renaissance, though the large flat hat with the liripipe is of the late Gothic period, still at that time in fashion. The liripipe tail itself is wound around the shoulders, hangs down the back and is attached to the waist belt. The patterned fabrics were pictorial in design. The shirt became important in fashion, reaching halfway down the thighs and slit at the sides, long sleeved but without a collar. The doublet with the laced sleeves allowed the white linen shirt to be visible along the underside of the arm, and could be seen around the armhole, since the sleeves were detachable and laced to the doublet with points or fasteners. The tabard-style men's costume only reached down to the thigh and was fur trimmed. The multi-coloured hose was made of patches of fabric, wide at the top and sewn together to form one garment. A cod-piece was always attached. The heel-less soft shoes were slightly elongated at the toes.

ELIZABETHAN COSTUME

This design is after the famous Spanish painter, Sanchez Coello of Alexander Farnese, grandson of Charles V. The detail taken from this source shows the cloak with hanging sleeves, slung in the fashionable way across one shoulder. The cloak has a high collar and is notched into the lapel. The doublet beneath has an even higher neckline, Spanish style, from which comes the ruff edge. The tunic could be sleeveless, with slightly protruding shoulder wings, fastened down the front by a close row of buttons. The skirt of the doublet could be short or deep. The sleeves were often of a different material, but were always long to the wrist, ending in a ruffle. The trunk hose were padded to give a stiff, rigid effect. They were slashed to show a coloured lining, the slashings often arranged to form a pattern. The black and white sketch shows the puffed-out hose with tights and the slashed tie-up shoe.

Altogether an impressive costume to suit a Shakespearian nobleman.

LATE ELIZABETHAN
COSTUME

This design is after a painting of around 1600 and is suitable for a character in many of Shakespeare's plays. The clothes are of a formal attire in the late Elizabethan period. The stiff doublet is padded and the skirts pointed at the waist. The hose or breeches reach the upper thighs and the tapering canion fall to the knees, over which long white woollen stockings are pulled. The short cloak, Spanish style, is heavily embroidered along the hem and edges. The neck ruff is starched and the shoes are slashed and fasten with lacing. Sword and gloves are carried.

DESIGNING FOR DICKENS

DICKENSIAN COSTUMES

It is always the work of a designer to 'dress' every character in the play, whether they have a speaking part or whether they just walk on. Costumes left to the actors' own or other people's ideas might well spoil the concept of the scene. So it is good practice to oversee every costume. The three characters illustrated here are designed for a Dickensian or any play set in the middle of the nineteenth century. The lady is in a travelling outfit with two capes, with slits for the arms. The head covering is the universal bonnet. This is formed when the crown and brim merge forming an almost horizontal line across the top. The sides of the brim curve down over the ears, forming an oval frame to the face. The bonnet strings come down across the brim to be tied under the chin. The man is wearing a single-breasted thigh-length jacket. The tight-fitting trousers are worn with instep straps. He sports a large scarf around the neck, and wears a shirt with a high stiffened collar. The long Chesterfield top coat has large lapels and a collar. Tall top hats were the popular style.

The design for the small girl follows the period fashion, her coat falling to below the knees, with a frilled hem, and around the shoulders a small fur-trimmed cape. White lace-edged cambric drawers show below the hem of the coat, reaching the ankles. Pump-type shoes are worn. The bonnet, worn towards the back of the head, is secured by a ribbon which emerges from inside the bonnet to fasten around the chin in a bow. Ringlets were popular. Fur muffs were carried.

FAGIN

As with all character designing, the designer should have a good, or at least a basic, knowledge of stage make up. This can add greatly to the effectiveness of the design: and Fagin is such a character. He must look dirty and unkempt, and be recognised immediately by the audience and not just unpleasant, but downright evil. The hip-length waistcoat is tied around the middle with a leather belt. Many of the buttons are missing. The ragged knee-length breeches are without knee fasteners and are left hanging loosely, with tatty ends. The long black stockings are also full of holes, and his shoes scruffy and untied. The calf-length greatcoat is also ragged, with the shirt sleeves protruding from the elbows. The grubby shirt has a scraggy necktie tied into a bow. The hair or wig is lank and greasy and covered with a black skull cap. The face should have a darkish make up to emphasize the hooked nose and scraggy beard, which depict Fagin's Eastern ancestry.

FAGIN'S DEN

As space was limited for this production it was necessary to convey the spirit of the scene on a cloth, without wings or borders, the sides being masked by curtains. The painted effect of light coming from the right carries the eye to a particular part of the stage – the table with all the stolen loot. Almost as effective as a fully built stage set, and a lot cheaper to make and quicker to paint!

OLIVER

More often than not the designer's work has to do more than create the outward show of clothes; these clothes have also to establish the character's personality. In designing Oliver, as opposed to Fagin or any other character in the play, the designer has to counterpoint for the audience the wickedness and evil of Fagin and his friends. In Oliver you must show that here is a good, wholesome and innocent boy, quite different from the evil Fagin and his friends, the butt of all the others' wickedness. The ragged workhouse costume can be made to suit your purpose well. The physique of the character is important – small, slim and waiflike. A white (or almost white) shirt is tucked into skimpy long trousers, patched, with holes and ragged bottoms. The double-breasted, waist-length coat has ragged cuffs and the shirt protrudes from the elbows. A skimpy scarf is tied around the neck. The stockings should hang around the dilapidated shoewear. The design depicts the scene when Oliver asks for more soup.

DAVID COPPERFIELD AND MR MICAWBER

Here are two characters from Charles Dickens' *David Copperfield*. Wearing the monocle and 'waiting for something to turn up' is Mr Micawber. The ideal actor for this part is someone tall who can be padded out over the stomach. The jacket under the top coat has a high collar and lapels. The shirt collar should be stiffened and high to accommodate the bowed cravat. The thigh-length frock coat is very tight fitting over the padded stomach, double-breasted with two side pockets. The straight sleeves have deep cuffs. The trousers are just below the knees and very close fitting, with the white stockings well exposed between them and slipper shoes. A grey top hat is worn.

David Copperfield's costume follows the Eton suit style worn by schoolboys of the day. The jacket is short and double-breasted, the front square cut with wide lapels. The back comes to a slight point at the centre, worn with a wide, starched, turned down collar and a single-breasted waistcoat. Trousers almost reach the ankles. A top hat is the usual headdress.

A CHRISTMAS CAROL ⌐

SCROOGE

Scrooge is a difficult character to design, as you have to think of three characters in one. Firstly, a mean, penny-pinching miser, secondly, a frightened and lonely old man who becomes contrite after the visitations, and thirdly the generous and happy individual who abounds with goodwill towards all men. Apart from the opening and closing scenes where he wears the outdoor clothes of the period, Scrooge is dressed in his night clothes.

So the designer must produce a complex character with the aid of good make up. Dressed in an ankle-length nightshirt over which he wears a long dressing gown, fastened in the centre by two buttons, he wears a thick woollen scarf around his neck which reaches his knees. The nightcap has a long tail with a white pompon at the tip. The bedroom slippers are brown. Make up is the main feature of this design, the face etched with hard, mean lines, gradually softening as the play proceeds. A study of make up should be a part of the designer's knowledge. Properties such as a candlestick holder add to the characterisation.

MARLEY

The designing of any supernatural figure, such as Marley, is always somewhat of a problem. If it is not well presented it will lose the desired effect. The design is best accomplished with the aid of the lighting expert, and it helps to be well-versed in the art of make up. The figure is dressed in the period, with a single-breasted frock coat and long trousers. A cravat and lace cuffs are also seen. The garments must be dyed, painted or sprayed in a light blue, as are the cash boxes hung around the body. The boxes themselves must be made of a light material: shoe boxes linked to simulated chains in the same light blue are ideal. The face should be made up in black, blue and green, and the hair or wig is best powdered in white or pale blue. The presentation of Marley's visitation should, where possible, be behind a gauze in a picture frame over the fireplace, or in a wall panel. The figure should be illuminated with white or blue from the bottom, using the light to give the desired ghostly effect.

Musicals, Opera and Dance

DESIGNING FOR MUSICALS

THE MIKADO

These designs are for the Gilbert and Sullivan D'Oyly Carte operetta, *The Mikado*. Over the years many famous designers have produced wonderful costumes for *The Mikado*, each a masterpiece of its time. In the 1920s the designer Charles Rickett designed a most successful production. He actually stencilled Japanese patterns on the leading costumes himself.

Here the designs have been approached in a traditional manner, redrawing directly from Japanese art work and wood prints, matching as closely as possible the delicate pale colouring so beloved by Japanese artists. The problem was to avoid making it all look too serious; after all, it is a light musical comedy operetta. Everyone was dressed in pale colours except the Mikado himself. Illustrated on the left is the figure of Nanki-Poo dressed in a short, tattered kimono with coloured legwear fastened at the knee and ankle. He carries a guitar and clutches a bundle of ballads. He wears a large straw hat fastened under the chin.

KO-KO

The character of Ko-Ko posed a problem. The performer is always depicted as small in stature, so he must be designed accordingly. Ko-Ko is in fact a cheap tailor who has been elevated to the exalted rank of Lord High Executioner. In keeping with Japanese art work and in order to retain authenticity, blending the comic figure, the idea was to dress him in the costume of a Samurai. This costume brings out the character of a little strutting man swathed in his Samurai armoured skirt. The armour effect is achieved by simulating strips of metal plates or bamboo strips held together with lacing. This is worn over a loose, just below the knees, kimono. A large sword is carried, allowing the actor to make comedy play by constantly tripping over it. The large hat and the holding of his 'little list of people' he would like to execute complete the costume.

THE MIKADO

The design of the Mikado must be in direct contrast to Ko-Ko. Here the physique of the actor is important. A thin weedy character would be out of place. The design has to be strikingly different, to fit a large man with overall authority. The costume shown here is a combination of kimono and hakama, a wide trouser-like garment, similar to culottes. Large shoulder pieces are worn over a black kimono. The Eboshi cap is a lacquered ceremonial headwear, very striking in appearance. The short white tabi stockings and heel-less sandals are authentically Japanese. He carries two swords to complete the picture of power and authority.

GUARD AND KATISHA

The design for the guard was built upon a samurai warrior. It features the kataginu, a sleeveless overgarment, tied with a sash and pulled up to the knees. The arms and legs are covered with armour. He carries two swords and a spear. Katisha's design was taken from a Japanese woodcut after Eisen. The kimono is a long gown with expansive sleeves set at right angles. It has no buttons or ties and is worn lapped left over right, crossed over the chest and secured at the waist with a wide sash, or obi, which is wound around twice finishing at the back in a large trailing bow. The obi is striped and decorated with the phoenix. Original Japanese designs are so numerous that almost any modern copy can be made to look stunning. The formal coiffure is perhaps best hired, or can be made by gathering the hair up and tying at the crown, adding a little false hair, with the tip folded forward. A chignon is formed by spreading out the hair. Ornamental bars and combs are added. The face is painted white, and the mouth made to look smaller by putting a red spot in the centre of the lower lip.

THE MIKADO SET

The backcloth depicting Mount Fuji conveys the spirit and location of the scene, with the assistance of wings, illustrated separately. These open wings are decorative and conventional in design, but unreal and imaginative in character.

The wings are of course built to the same scale as the backcloth, so that when placed in front they focus attention on the action in the foreground.

HMS PINAFORE

HMS Pinafore is one of Gilbert and Sullivan's most loved musical comedies, performed time and again by amateur and professional companies. Designs need to be bright and cheerful, in essence expressing the feel of the production.

The costume here is for the handsome Ralph Rackstraw, the character sadly in love with the captain's daughter, Josephine; but the basic uniform design could be for all the sailors in the play. As this is the costume of a Victorian sailor, the actual uniform will need to be made, the chances of any originals still being available in a surplus store being most improbable. The high waisted flap-front trousers have large bell-bottoms. The shirt is loose fitting with a large blue collar with three white stripes. The jacket is waist length with short turned back lapels. The straw hat is low crowned and wide brimmed. The neckerchief and the long-tailed hatband are black. Shoe styles are optional, either black leather or black pumps.

ANNA AND THE KING OF SIAM

Designing for this play posed many problems. The decision was to costume the King in the uniform of a Royal Palace Guard, as this was a mixture of East and West. The black velvet hat is completely Eastern in character. The tunic, in European style, is worn in either blue or white. The adornments are very colourful, collar and cuffs being of pink fabric and the belt purple with gold lace. What appears to be knee breeches is in fact a loin cloth, called a panung, and made of silk, usually about 60cm/2ft wide and 2m/7ft long. The ends are passed between the legs and drawn up at the back, forming pantaloons, culotte shape. The loin cloth has a deep gold edging (see sketch of the method used).

The Siamese dancer is designed from the actual garments. The skirt, similar to the men's, is a straight length of fabric, about 90cm/3ft long. This is wrapped around the body, laid into groups of pleats, and fastened with a belt. The colours of green and red are quite stunning. The pagoda-style metal hat is covered in gilt and dazzling stones.

KISS ME KATE

Here is a complex scene made more difficult by the very small stage area available. The opening scene shows an empty stage with a back wall. It then has to open up to reveal the set of the play. As both scenes are in constant use, it was designed so that

the 'stage back wall' would open to reveal the painted backcloth of the set. This is achieved by the actors unfolding and changing the sets themselves. See also pages 38 and 39 for designs for *The Taming of the Shrew*.

SOUTH PACIFIC

This musical is set on a Pacific island during the Second World War. The personnel are American service men and women. This is a case of hiring rather than making. Most surplus stores stock these or similar uniforms. The design shows an American naval petty officer in his 'whites', the tropical dress uniform of the American naval enlisted men. The cap, tunic, jumper and trousers are white. The blue collar and cuffs are bordered with three white stripes. The shoes are of black leather. On the left arm is a P.O. rating badge. The eagle patch is white, the stripes or chevrons (inverted, as per American regulations) and the machinist's propeller patch are red. The neckerchief is black. The design of the service woman is that of a chief nurse, US Army Nurse Corps 1943. She is a lieutenant junior graded and the single silver bar of that rank is worn on the right shirt collar. The Nurse Corps oakleaf and anchor insignia in gilt is worn as a crown badge on the white-topped cap with its gilt chin strap mounted at the top edge of the black mohair band. The Corps badge is repeated on the left shirt collar. The stripe-and-a-half of this rank is worn in gold on the blue shoulder boards. Much of this fine detail could be omitted.

NIGHT CLUB

Night club scenes feature
in all sorts of plays,
musicals and revues, giving
the designer opportunities
to produce something
exciting and dramatic. This
American night club shows
the cut-out buildings of
the city in the background,
illuminated from below.
The trestled wall ground
row has lighted ornamental
lamps. The two trestled
wing pieces, shown
separately, have candle
lights. Tables and chairs are
required for this scene.

GUYS AND DOLLS ⌣

NIGHT CLUB, HAVANA

This design is made for dancing against a cyclorama. A centre set piece of a fountain and the two side open wings indicate the Havana setting: the lit-up sign 'Nite Club Havana' will leave the audience in no doubt as to the location. The lighting should give a warm, orange glow.

MISSION HALL

Designs for this production ought to suggest a mood of reality. The design here was for a scene in which it was necessary to convey the idea on a cloth, without the assistance of wings or borders. This is often called a front cloth, and allows the following scene, for instance the interior of the mission hall, to be set up behind it while the preceding scene is still in progress. Lighting can unify the picture by using a single tonal effect of colour.

SEWER

This is a design for two cloths, one hung behind the other. It has to be painted and lit to convey the impression of dull dankness. The single lights are to represent a certain gloominess. The card playing scene within the sewers is played centre stage, lit to create a centre of interest, focusing on this spot to concentrate attention on the action.

SOUTH AMERICAN SET

This was designed for a musical number with singers and dancers. It is a light fanciful scene, and calls for both delicate and striking colours. The pink of the walls and buildings are in contrast to the colours of the drapery and cacti. The warm orange background suggests the tone of the play. A too realistic setting would leave nothing to the imagination. The set allows plenty of room for dancers and actors to move freely.

THE DESERT

Any number of musicals and plays seem to end up at some point or another in the desert, calling for a simple but effective desert scene. The backcloth must be designed to show a vastness of space – as far as the eye can see. The near distance can be relieved by trees. The wings, illustrated separately, are painted to represent the walls of desert forts or houses. A simple set like this allows plenty of stage area in which the actors may move freely.

Pygmalion -

Doolittle

The character of Doolittle is designed here for the opening scenes of the play, *Pygmalion*, or the musical, *My Fair Lady*. The left hand figure shows the dress of a dustman (or refuse collector, if you must) of the period. The fan-tailed hat protects his neck and shoulders from the refuse container when hoisted on his shoulders. The shirt, possibly ex-army, is striped and buttoned up at the neck. A red neckerchief is worn, probably as a sweat rag. The hard wearing, coarse trousers are caught at the knees by strings and supported by braces and a leather belt around the waist. In contrast, the figure on the right depicts the very same Doolittle in the transformed person of a 'gentleman', dressed in his formal wedding suit. The grey tailcoat has a single centre fastening and wide lapels. Beneath this coat he wears a double-breasted waistcoat in a contrasting colour, with a spotted cravat and simple pin. Spats are worn over the shoes. The hair is in the popular style of the period with centre parting and a curled moustache.

ELIZA DOOLITTLE

A Covent Garden flower girl, characteristic of the time before the First World War, is here depicted in the typical garments worn by the poor of London: a striped shirt blouse and a shabby woollen skirt reaching the ankles, a white apron, a mark of respectability, a ragged woollen scarf worn around the neck. Over this outfit the three-quarter-length coat looks as though it has seen better days. She has a round, crowned straw hat with a flat brim and black hatband, and wears black stockings and well-worn ankle-high boots. She invariably carries a basket of flowers. The transformation of Eliza from flower girl to a lady shows a close-fitting, sleeved white crêpe-de-Chine evening gown with a deep decolletage, a large chiffon rosette attached at the waist. The evening wrap is of red velvet with a black fur trim. A tiara and pearl necklace complete the elegant picture.

PYGMALION ~·

PORTER AND FLOWER GIRL

The design shows typical street characters for either the play or the musical. On the left is a Covent Garden porter wearing an almost knee length, double-breasted jacket with a high-lapelled single-breasted waistcoat, and the popular 'choker' tied into a bow around his neck. The loose-fitting trousers are caught up with string just below the knees. Heavy boots are usually worn. The hard felt tall crowned hat with the brim curled up at the sides is known as a bowler. He always carries a red handkerchief, either sticking out of a pocket or wound around the neck.

The figure on the right, a flower girl, is seen here wearing an ankle-length coat, well worn, and a small scarf. Underneath she is wearing a black skirt and an apron. Over her shoulders a checked shawl falls down to the hips. She is wearing black stockings and ankle-high laced boots. Over her hair, parted in the centre, she is wearing a low-crowned, wide-brimmed straw hat with ribbon bows. Her whole appearance is dull and shoddy.

DOMESTIC SERVANTS

There is hardly a drawing room comedy or whodunnit that does not involve the domestic staff in the dastardly goings-on: those were the days. Here I show three staple types of stage domestics. The popular maid, so often seen in the late 1920s and 30s, is wearing a black dress with white collar and cuffs and a little white apron. A small white cap or wide headband is usually worn. Stockings are usually black or grey, worn with black shoes. The uniformed chauffeur is seen here in a simple formal uniform, very effective with high gloss boots, gloves and peaked cap.

The famous 'French maid' is showing off her saucy low cut, thigh-length black dress with just the hint of the petticoat frill revealed at the hem. A very small white, frilly apron is tied around the waist. A flat headscarf is tied under the chin. Sheer silk stockings and high heeled mule-type shoes are equally essential elements in this traditionally sexy costume. No French farce worthy of the name is complete without one.

GARDEN BACKDROP

This is only part of a design, but figures in
many plays with an interior. The exterior
backdrop calls for both good design and good
lighting. The backcloth can be of an exterior,
buildings or gardens. It should be painted so
that distant objects are in soft focus, more
delicate colouring, and nearer objects
becoming stronger and clearer, more in focus.
This aids the perspective. A single tonal lighting
effect of overall colour, or white, conveys the
right impression.

FRENCH WINDOWS

Designed as an architectural reality, the french
windows must be firmly fixed and easy to
open and close. Pelmet boards and hanging
curtains, chosen for their blending of colours,
clearly have to match the rest of the set. This
scene must be lit from the appropriate
direction, depending on the time of day. As day
turns to night, or vice-versa, the source of
lighting needs to be altered to accommodate
this illusion.

DESIGNING FOR OPERA

CARMEN

This is a complete breakaway from opera's traditional costuming. The design adds a more modern approach, and also enhances the character of Carmen in a more visual and subtle way. The red dress is simple and slightly waisted with shoulder straps and a side slit to the thigh, revealing the lace-edged undergarment and the 1930s-style suspender belt supporting black net stockings. The hair is caught at the back in a hairnet bag and at the front falls in tight corkscrew curls to frame the face. The matador hat is placed at a jaunty angle and the decorated matador's coat is slung over the right shoulder. The shoes are red with large lace bows, fastened with a single jewel. The fan is large and made of almost transparent lace.

DIE WALKÜRE

Perhaps more than any other type of production, opera is highly costumed. The designs for the two characters illustrated here, Siegmund and Brunnhilde, are good examples of heavily costumed operatic figures. Both are dressed in the bizarre fashion of Northern gods and goddesses. With the usual large number of singers involved, all dressed in a great variety of different coloured costumes, an opera production can be a lavish visual spectacle. Make up is always an important complement to the skill of the costume designer, but especially so in colossal productions featuring dozens of different characters.

Madame Butterfly backcloth

This painted backcloth was greatly influenced by a famous nineteenth century Japanese woodblock colour print. It conveys, by its symbolic treatment and economy of colour, the atmosphere of both period and location. It is an idealised picture to give an emotional impression of the action on stage. Being an opera, the setting is always unreal and imaginative and must be presented to the audience as such.

MADAME BUTTERFLY

This interpretation of the character of Madame Butterfly is after an original design by Erté. This particular colourful design was made for a mannequin parade of showgirls. It was subsequently used with a few accessories for a solo number from the production. The plain white kimono is stencilled with a series of butterflies of varying sizes. Each sleeve is decorated with larger pointed butterflies. Three separate coloured collars represent the undergarments. The obi, or sash, is tied in front, falling into wings. White tabi or stockings are worn with the geta-type clogs. The large black wig, Japanese style, is decorated with combs and pins. A paper sun shade and fan are carried.

DESIGNING FOR BALLET AND DANCE

THE DYING SWAN

Arising from a request to move away from the traditional Pavlova costume, this is an interesting experimental design suitable for the solo dancer in both classical and modern ballet. The design shows the silk leotard and tights in one, and sprayed in a light blue. The feather wings are attached to the back and a close-fitting feathered swan head is worn. Round the waist is a ground-length chiffon skirt with a fine pliable wire along the lower edge. The material is sprayed a bluish green with silver highlights. The movement of the dance causes the skirt to swirl, representing the waves of water on the lake. At the climax the skirt is drawn over the whole body as the swan sinks to the ground. With correct lighting, this can be a most effective design.

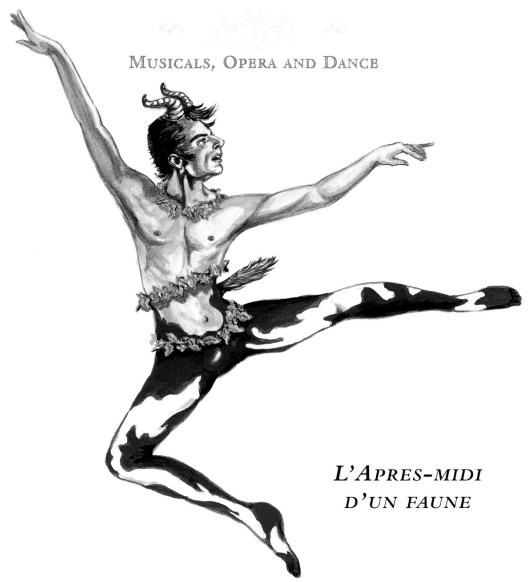

L'APRES-MIDI
D'UN FAUNE

This design for a dancer of *L'Après-midi d'un faune* was conceived after a design by Bakst for the dancer Nijinsky. Together with the Ballets Russe, Bakst audaciously showed the theatre how to flaunt accepted theatrical convention. His characteristic designs became the subject of enthusiastic emulation throughout the theatre world of Europe. Whereas Bakst used a body sock as the basic costume, this design is different and is based only on a leather pouch jockstrap, which is secured around the waist: experimentation is always a good trait for designers. In my original design, a fine pair of tights is worn over the pouch and fastened to the belt. The tights are first subject to being painted or sprayed with a brown and white motif. A tail piece is added to complete the costume. The second design dispenses with the tights; after the pouch is positioned, the legs to the waist are made up with stage make up. This is tedious, but very effective. The added green sprigs are purely symbolic to represent the forest.

PETROUCHKA

This costume for Petrouchka is after an original design by Benois, designed for Nijinsky. Ballet has always held a great fascination for the costume designer because of its languid sensuality. The tu-tu, and the long, full, white circular skirts of gauze or net, the tunic tops and clinging tights of the ballerinas are the concept of the traditional classical ballet. However, there are areas of classical ballet that allow the designer opportunities to create exotic, sumptuous and colourful designs against the background of traditional and classical costumes. The costume illustrated here shows characteristic combinations of colour in a striking design for the character of Petrouchka. The costume fabric is shown in rich and brilliant colours. A perfect co-ordination of theatre arts between dancer and designer brings Petrouchka, the puppet doll, to life.

CAT

Good stagecraft admits of no limits to the imagination; the designer is therefore free to create kings, clowns and animals, all to be on equal terms before the audience. This design is ideal for ballet and plays for both adults and children. The idea is simple and effective, using a leotard or body sock with long sleeves in a skin or grey colour, with a design either painted or sprayed on. A flexible tail of lightweight fur fabric is made and attached to the rear of the costume. The head is covered completely, leaving only the face visible. The head covering is treated in the same way as the body, being sprayed or painted in the chosen design. Ears are then cut out and sewn to the head covering. These are important as they are an integral part of the costume. A large bow can be worn around the neck. As this is an open-face mask, the face should be made up. The top half should be in a similar colour to the costume, with the eyes and the rest of the face in normal make up.

SHOWGIRL ❧ 1

Designing for revue, night-clubs, casinos and suchlike venues really brings out the bizarre and fanciful ideas in most designers. It was Leon Bakst's outrageously exotic sets and costumes that captured the imagination of other designers. He was followed and copied by his fellow artist Poiret, who responded to the gorgeous vitality of Bakst's line and colour. This costume, after a Paris Lido design of 1957, shows a showgirl in tasteful *déshabillé*, framed in the most artistic way by sumptuous drapery with which she seems to be only loosely connected. The ruched, trouser-type tights are elegant and seductive. The headdress, which creates height to add to the impression of elegance, consists of a complete head covering fastened under the chin, on which is erected the support for the horizontally held feathers. Body jewellery is attached at the shoulders, neck and waist by a jewelled girdle.

SHOWGIRL ⌣ 2

This is a design after Basil Crage, and coming from an age when nudes were not standard, is a showgirl costume truly astonishing in its modernity. The remarkable thing about the original is that it was designed in 1900, but has all the features of a more recent, modern costume. It must have been very daring and provocative in its time! The sheer sensuality of the whole costume, the scantily covered breast, the openings over the lower part of the stomach and thighs still take the breath away; the protruding side pieces with the hanging tassels and drapes highlight the whole colourful atmosphere of the costume. The crowning glory, the headwear, is close fitted, its high, curved side pieces giving added height. The trailing coloured feathers finish off this gorgeous costume.

SHOWGIRL ∼ 3

This design is for The Bluebell Girls performing at the Lido in Paris in the late 1950s. The excellence of the design is the obvious sensuality of simplicity and elegance. It shows a modest sexuality with the bikini in a lacy material with arm covering to just above the elbows. The feathers, both in the high head covering and held in the hand, add to the fantasy of the costume. This type of designing is very difficult, balancing theatricality with a barely concealed sexuality, and not allowing one to overwhelm the other. But what finer opportunity has the designer to costume the most perfect tall and elegant figure? The designer, however, must always remain conscious of the audience.

PUNK DANCERS

In this design for a dance routine, the couple are dressed in a variety of garments. The boy is wearing a loose spider knot jumper over a fragmented, slashed shirt. The faded denim jeans are ripped, worn with coloured socks and pumps. The hair is cut in a roach or Mohican style, dyed in a variety of colours and is shaven at the sides. The face can be painted with various embellishments. Chunky bracelets are worn. The design for the girl is not as extreme. The short buckled dress with a fringe at the hem is supported by thin shoulder straps. The hair is dyed blue, and brushed backwards to make it spiky. Second-hand clothes, dyed in various colours, are ideal for these costumes.

Pantomimes and Children's Plays

DESIGNING FOR PANTOMIME

CINDERELLA

Designing costumes for pantomime is always fun, with nothing to stop your imagination wandering from the traditional to the fantastic. In fact anything goes. Illustrated here is the transformation moment when Cinderella, the down-trodden kitchen girl, is, in seconds, changed into a lovely young woman in a beautiful evening gown. In the foreground design Cinders, sweeping the kitchen floor, is dressed in rags. Then, simply by waving her magic wand, the Fairy Godmother completes the dramatic transformation. Just off-stage the evening robe is laid on the ground with the hoops carefully placed one upon the other, with Cinders ready to step into the open dress, which is pulled up and fastened at the back with velcro. Her long-haired wig is removed and a powdered wig substituted, all in a moment. The evening gown is of the open robe style, with a tight close-fitting bodice and a low, round neckline, the buttons down the centre front tied by a 'bosom knot'. The elbow-length sleeves have double frills.

PANTOMIME KITCHEN

The big, warm kitchen effect is created by the impression of a huge beam and a large brick fireplace and oven. As much of the stage is taken up by the various antics of the actors, it is important to allow them the space they need around and in front of the scenery. The lighting must be bright to unify the scene in a single tone of colour.

PANTOMIME COOK

This character is always played by a man. The design is usually Victorian in origin, but it can be of almost any period and need follow no set pattern. It is fantasy burlesque with interchangeable fashions, though many of the actors who play these parts have definite ideas on how they should be dressed. My design here shows the large mob cap with a red wig, the gaudy dress well padded over the chest and stomach. A white bib apron is fastened over the shoulders and around the waist. This is an ideal costume for kitchen scenes. Bright striped stockings and buckled shoes complete the picture.

VILLAGE SCENE

This type of village scene is exclusively pantomime, and used mainly as an opening scene to introduce the cast. The design follows the storybook style in being strikingly colourful, decorative and imaginative.

HI PONG

Pantomime has many different characters. Nowadays many of the Eastern legends – *Arabian Nights, Aladdin, Ali Baba* and *Sinbad the Sailor* – are mixed together to produce one story. Illustrated here is the cobbler character, Hi Pong. The design follows the traditional spirit of a gaudy costume, yellow shirt with long sleeves, full baggy trousers to the calf, striped stockings and Eastern turned-up slippers. A cobbler's brown bib-style apron with a centre fastening, the tails hanging down the back, is also worn. A very tall red fez adds considerably to the overall effect.

ALADDIN

Following the tradition of pantomime Aladdin, the principal boy, is played by a woman. The usual court dress for Aladdin is a sumptuously full garment, but the Chinese/Japanese kimono style shows a more modern approach. The kimono is full and wide, the sleeves long with a wide opening. The garment is knee length, caught up in the front, in a draped effect. A long knotted sash with long flowing ties is placed around the waist. The high-necked undergarment crosses over at the chest. The hat is somewhere between the Chinese round hat and a Japanese style of hat decoration. Pointed Eastern-style slippers are worn.

ALADDIN'S CAVE

This set has to convey the impression of mystery. The rugged wall of the cave gives an atmosphere of impending menace. Lighting is important as it can enhance the picture by using different tones, sometimes darkening the background, sometimes emphasizing particular objects such as the treasure. Lighting can be used imaginatively to create different centres of interest as each scene moves along.

GENIE OF THE LAMP

Designs for the Genie of the Lamp in *Aladdin* can range from the bizarre to the fantastic. The audience expect something unusual to appear, and the designer must not disappoint them. The design must be colourful with a touch of humour. A tall fez hat, a bright shirt with a short sleeveless bolero-type jacket and large patterned baggy pantaloons and a very wide striped sash around the waist make an effective costume. Slippers could be with turned-up toes. A small black beard could complete the make up.

GENIE OF THE RING

According to Arabic legend genies were powerful spirits, some good, some evil. Designing the Genie of the Ring, as opposed to the Genie of the Lamp, calls for a different approach. This Genie, although also fantastic and bizarre, but in a different way, is powerful and terrifying. He wears three garments: one is an ankle-length sleeveless wrap-over type of garment, brightly coloured with another, black, sleeveless jacket down to the calf. Under these the undergarment has very large and wide sleeves. A very wide sash with hanging tails is around the waist, with a long scimitar dagger inserted. The collar should be round and wide, reaching the shoulders. The pointed fez with a wide upright brim is decorated with feathers and crescents. The slippers are Eastern in style, with turned-up toes. Make up should be darkened, and a black forked beard helps create the character.

PRINCESS NUMA

The design for Princess Numa, as for all pantomime characters, must be colourful, regardless of authenticity. The gown designed here is ground length, falling in folds with wide sleeves caught at the elbows and wrists, where they are fastened with hanging ribbons. Over the dress is a high-necked thigh-length tabard, the four corners decorated with tassels. The waist is encircled in a sash. The hat is tall, widening at the top and decorated either side with muslin or gauze bows. Heel-less slippers are worn.

THE SULTAN

This character can be benign or evil, depending on the script, but in either case the costume has to be designed for a high exalted individual. The long undergarment has long full sleeves of a contrasting colour. The wide fur collar covers the shoulders and falls down the front. The headwear is very ornate, high in the front with a central decoration of stiffened parts extending wide across the face. The slippers have turned-up toes.

MARKET SCENE

The centre piece of the Ali Baba market scene is designed against a cyclorama illuminated in a warm orange colour. The centre piece retains the feeling of a market place. The movements of the actors on stage, called paths of action, are a vital part of the stage workings, so there must also be space behind the centre piece. This is not a still picture, but works as a real place in which actors must move.

WIDOW TWANKEY ~ HOUSE CLOTHES

The character of Widow Twankey, a poor washer woman and the mother of Aladdin, is the traditional comedy part, the Dame, and as usual is played by a man. The material wretchedness and poverty of the character must be indicated, but nevertheless in bright and cheerful colours. A garish green doublet is worn over the long-sleeved, bright yellow blouse. This is fastened down the front with thonging. The full-length, wide skirt is a light brown, and appears ragged and well patched. The dirty white apron also has patches. A red shawl is draped over the shoulders and knotted at the front. The whole costume must be well padded, especially across the bust. The wig should appear scraggy and very untidy with a thin headband. Make up should be the usual red nose type; but it should not disguise the fact that the character is played by a man only pretending to be a woman.

WIDOW TWANKEY ~ BALL DRESS

In contrast to the original appearance of this character, this design must convey her wondrous accession to the world of unlimited riches, not to mention everlasting bliss. The Japanese and Chinese styles are mixed. The long kimono with the open centre is greatly padded at the back and chest. The kimono is gathered at the waist by a broad ribbon belt fastening in a bow at the front. The large hanging sleeves are in a contrasting colour of black, with a red lining. The hair is dressed in the Japanese style, tied near the crown, making a loop to stand upright. The remainder of the hair hangs loosely down the back and is decorated with ribbon bows and flowers.

MUMTEZ,
SERVANT OF ABANAZER

Here is a design for an unpleasant servant, who serves an equally unpleasant Abanazer. Being a pantomime character, he must appear in colourful garments, but he needs to have an air of cringing servitude; evidently an obnoxious individual. The undergarment reaches to just below the knees, with full sleeves tapering to the wrists where they end with cuffs. The fully-ornamented outer garment is sleeveless, with a high standing collar. The headwear is a round Chinese cap with a black bow and red top. Eastern-type slippers encase the feet.

ABANAZER

All pantomimes have their villain, and one favourite such character is Abanazer, who must appear to be the personification of evil. The design has to show all this evil, evident to the audience at first sight. The undergarment should be a dull red, long to the ankles, fastened with a black sash and with full wide sleeves. The voluminous cape should reach the ground and be fastened high at the chest, with a bright red lining. The headwear should be large, with a full tail hanging down the back, the front of which is a full, stiffened, rolled brim framing the face. The stockings are green and the shoes black, with long pointed toes. Make up should be dark, with a black beard and alarming moustache.

RED RIDING HOOD

The eponymous heroine of the pantomime is preferably played by a youngish actress, sometimes even a teenager, not too tall, but always with a good singing voice. It should not be too difficult to design this costume, consisting mainly of a blouse and a simple nondescript skirt of any period. The important garment is the red cape, usually of three-quarter length with a hood large enough partially to cover the head and face. This is of great significance, as the wolf must wear the same or a similar garment in the well known cottage scene.

WOLF

Designing animal characters falls into two basic categories. The actor may be able to play his part in a normal, upright human position, walking on two legs; or he may be limited to moving about on all fours, more like the animal he portrays. Here the design is for an 'upright' animal, and in this instance it is the headmask that reveals the animal's identity. Realism is needed as far as the mask is concerned, as the other part of the costume is pure fantasy. The mask may be hired, but a good property person can make a realistic mask. The same fur fabric used for the mask can be used for the leg covering and the tail. A large frock coat and waistcoat can complete the costume. With the addition of high boots, a hat, gloves and a walking stick this looks very effective.

ROBIN HOOD

A mixture of period styles is acceptable for pantomimes, audiences being impressed more by effect than authenticity and not looking for realism in this kind of theatre. Robin Hood is always acted by a female. This design is almost mediaeval in concept, though with a modern approach. The doublet and trunks, in one, is open at the neck with a short lapel. The front and sides are closed with thonging. A belt with a small money bag attached encircles the waist. Flesh coloured tights are worn with high to-the-knee leather boots. The high crowned hat has a deep brim which is turned up at the sides, coming to a narrow point in the front. The whole costume is leaf green.

WITCH

Here is a character that can appear in any number of productions, from pantomime to children's plays and ballet. The design shows a witch easily adapted to be either a good or a wicked witch. Care should be exercised when designing the latter, as too frightening a witch can upset the audience, especially the younger members. Too pedestrian, however, and the character is lost. It is a difficult task because all ages look at the designer's art, but they all see something different. Design a witch with a dark brown hat and a short cloak, and in amber lighting the hat will appear brown and the short cloak will not hide the figure. The skirt and coloured stockings can be seen, and the witch is thus not frightening. If the lighting is changed to blues and greens, the whole costume becomes dark and sinister. A longer cloak can be added. The face can be made up in a light green, which is not too sinister unless seen in dark lighting. The final effect of this design depends very much on the lighting.

DESIGNING FOR CHILDREN'S PLAYS

BEE

Children's costumes should be designed with as much care as any other. Children are actors, just like the adult performers, and share the stage with them. The way they are costumed is just as important to the success of the production. Firstly, their costumes must be simple and comfortable, neither clumsy nor heavy. The leotard is a very useful garment and can be applied in many effective ways. In this design, which represents a bee, whether realistic or fantasy, the designer has to make a reasonable representation, or at least a recognisable one, of the way a bee actually looks. A fur fabric of a base colour was selected as the most suitable to represent the colour of a bee, and this was coloured by dyeing and painting. A larger fitting leotard was chosen which was then padded out just under the chest line to just below the stomach. The padding must be just right, just enough to give the look and feel of a bee's plump body. The second part of the body was then cut out and sewn together and firmly padded. The two parts were then firmly sewn together, with no sagging. The wings could be of a shape cut out of a stiff buckram or a wire frame draped over with silk or chiffon and then sewn. The finished wings were then attached to the upper back of the leotard. The headmask can be completed in papier mache to fit the head, with 'feelers' and eyes attached and painted. The sketches show padding of the leotard and the fixture of the wings.

BEEHIVE SCENE

This is real theatrical
fantasy. The cloth painting
is bold, larger than life,
unreal and imaginative.
The Alice in Wonderland
effect is achieved by the
sheer vastness of the design
and the great splashes of
colour. Whether children
or adults dance or act
against this background,
they will be transformed
into a world of make-
believe, a world of delicate
and striking colours.

ELF

Designing for children is always a problem, especially when fairies or elves are involved. The question always arises as to what exactly is a fairy or an elf. The answer must be what you imagine it to be, but you have to design a vision that is purely symbolic fantasy. The designer is torn between reality and fantasy, moving from one to the other. A world of fairies is more romantic than mundane everyday life, so the designer must speak to children and adults alike in a classic dream of escape. The elf is a wild uncontrollable spirit, nice, but also destructive. The technique is to design something highly stylistic, interpreting the quality of lightness in the flowing fabrics of the costume. The greenish undergarment and leg covering is contrasted with the brownish overtunic with wide sleeves and billowing tails. The pointed green hat has hanging side pieces with large ears attached. The only colour, apart from the earth colours, is that of the red pointed slipper shoes. Paradoxically fairies and elves have outlasted changing fashion and still survive today, and have a vitality, for good or bad.

NATIVITY ~
MARY AND JOSEPH

This is perhaps one of the most difficult types of play to design. It is so easy to fall into the old style of Eastern dress when presenting the birth of Christ; and audiences find it difficult to accept a symbolic approach to this subject. These costumes, whilst breaking away from the stereotype, still retain an air of the traditional: the figures of Joseph and Mary, not in Eastern garb, are dressed in a more Western style, in fact in early Roman peasant attire. Mary is wearing a short-sleeved tunic over a white linen undertunic or shift. Her head covering is achieved with a fold of her rectangular cloak or palla drawn over her head. She is carrying a naked child. Joseph is wearing a simple loose-fitting, knee-length tunic with a belt around the waist. The trousers are stuffed into the soft leather boots. A stave was often carried when walking.

NATIVITY SCENE

Suggestion and simplicity are the keynotes of good design; too much decoration often results in confusion. In front of a simple backcloth is a symbolic outline of the stable that housed the Holy Family. Well positioned lighting conveys the illusion that the painted moon on the backcloth illuminates the cradle where the infant baby lies. The colour of the set can be enhanced by bringing up certain colours directly on to the straw and suppressing others in the surrounding areas.

NATIVITY BACKCLOTH

This is a backcloth for a very small stage. The star is seen, bright and unmistakable, highlighted against a black sky. The symbolic use of trees to the right conveys an impression of location – Bethlehem. This background, suitably adjusted, can be used for other productions.

GLOSSARY

Alb Priest's long white tunic.
Apron Decorative feature, worn over a skirt.

Backcloth Scenic canvas battened top and bottom, the width of the stage.
Bakst, Leon 1866-1924. Costume designer.
Benois, Alexandre Twentieth century stage designer.
Bliaut Close-fitting garment of the twelfth to early fourteenth century; worn by both sexes.
Bluebell Girls Group of showgirls.

Canions Decorative frills to the top of stockings, worn with the petticoat breeches fashion.
Carpaccio, Vittore 1455-1526. Venetian painter.
Chesterfield Overcoat named after the Earl of Chesterfield; 1830s–40s, then until the end of the century.
Chignon Hair at the back of the head arranged in loops or ringlets; second half of the eighteenth century.
Choker Scarf-like neckwear.
Cod-piece Front flap of the hose forming a pouch at the fork; fifteenth to sixteenth century.
Copotain Hat with a high conical crown with a narrow brim.
Corselet Short front laced jacket.
Crage, Basil Twentieth century stage costume designer.
Cravat Neckcloth or tie.
Culottes Split skirt; worn as shorts.
Cummerbund Wide waist sash.

Dalmatica Garment shaped like a cross with a slit for the neck opening.
Decolletage Low neckline of a lady's dress.
Doublet Short-style man's jacket; close fitting and tight waisted; fourteenth to seventeenth centuries.

Eboshi cap Laquered ceremonial headwear.
Eisen, Keisai 1790-1848. Japanese artist.

Erté (Romain de Tirtoff) 1892-1990. Russian born, Paris based fashion and theatre designer. Twentieth century.
Eton suit Morning coat worn by boys of Eton College.

Fez Brimless cap, a truncated cone shape.
Frock coat Close-fitting male coat, buttoned to the waist with hanging tails at the back; end of the eighteenth to end of the nineteenth centuries.

Gee-gaws Old word for jewellery of various types.
Geta Japanese sandal type of clog.
Girdle Belt.
Greaves Metal or leather leggings.
Groundrow Low piece of cut-out scenery.

Hakama Wide trouser-like attire, similar to culottes.
Halberd Long-staffed axe weapon used in the fifteenth and sixteenth centuries.

Jerkin Loose jacket or doublet.

Kataginu Sleeveless overgarment.
Kimono Loose gown tied around the waist with a sash and wide sleeves.

Leotard Practice costume of ballet dancers; similar to a body stocking.
Libas Cotton pantaloons.
Lido, Paris Glamour show theatre.
Liripipe Hooded cape with a long pendant tailpiece; 1350 to the end of the fifteenth century.
Lorica segmentata Metal body armour.

Mohican Hairstyle worn by North American Indians. Popular punk fashion 1970s.

Nijinsky, Vaslav 1890-1950. Famous ballet dancer of Polish origin.

Obi Wide very long sash, Japanese. Worn with kimono.

Palla Roman lady's voluminous cloak held on each shoulder by a fibula or brooch.
Pantaloons Long, tight or baggy trousers.
Pantomime Typically English Christmas entertainment.
Panung Wrapped breeches of Thailand.
Papier mache Method of using strips of paper pasted and applied into a mould or over an object.
Points Ties used to attach male trunk-hose to doublet and female sleeves to gowns.
Poiret, Paul 1879-1944. Paris born costume designer.
Punk Cult of bizarre, aggressively dressed young people. 1970s.

Ruff Circular collar of cambric or linen with a goffered frill; 1560s–1640s.

Shendyt Egyptian type of kilt, principal garment for men, long scarf wrapped around hips and held in place by a belt.
Slashings Symmetrical arrangement of slits in various lengths, with pulled through lining as decoration.

Tabard Rectangular length of fabric with centre slit for the head; worn by both sexes over a tunic. Twelfth century.
Tabi Japanese cotton foot mitten.
Toga Large piece of material wrapped around the body; worn by Romans of both sexes.
Trews Celtic breeches.
Trunk hose Male breeches from waist to thigh; 1550s–1610.
Tunica Short garment worn by the Greeks and Romans.
Tu-tu Gauze or net ballet skirt.

Velcro Hooked strips of nylon tape attached to material, when pressed together holds together.

Wings Curtains or pieces of scenery either side of the stage.

BIBLIOGRAPHY

Allardyce, N. *The Development of the Theatre*, George Harrap, London, 1927

Arnold, J. *Patterns of Fashion* (Vols. 1–3), Macmillan, London, 1972–85

Barton, L. *Historic Costume for the Stage*, Boston, Mass., 1938; A. & C. Black, London, 1961

Barton, L. *Period Patterns*, A. & C. Black, London, 1970

Bradfield, N. *Historical Costumes of England 1066–1968*, Harrap, London, 1970

Brooke, I. *Costume in Greek Classical Drama*, Theatre Arts, New York, NY, 1965

Brooke, I. *Medieval Theatre Costume*, A. & C. Black, London, 1967

Cassin-Scott, J. *Costumes and Settings for Historical Plays* (Vols 1–5), B. T. Batsford, London, 1979

Cassin-Scott, J. *The Amateur Dramatics Handbook*, Cassell, London, 1992

Cassin-Scott, J. *The Illustrated Encyclopaedia of Costume and Fashion*, Studio Vista, London, 1994

Corson, R. *Stage Make-up*, Peter Owen, London, 1960

Corson, R. *Fashions in Hair*, Peter Owen, London, 1985

Cunnington, C. W. and P. E and Beard, Charles *Dictionary of English Costume 900–1900*, A. & C. Black, London, 1974

Cunnington, P. *Costumes of Household Servants*, A. & C. Black, London, 1974

Cunnington, P. and Lucas, C. *Occupational Costume*, A. & C. Black, London, 1967

Cunnington, P. and Mansfield, A. *Handbook of English Costume in the 20th Century 1900–1960*, Faber & Faber, London, 1973

D'Amic, *Theater Art*, Manual Arts Press, Peoria, IL, 1931

Dorner, J. *Fashion in the Twenties and Thirties*, Ian Allan, Shepperton, 1973

Dorner, J. *Fashion in the Forties and Fifties*, Ian Allan, Shepperton, 1973

Earle, A. M. *Two Centuries of Costume in America 1620–1820 (2 vols.)*, Dover, New York, NY, 1970

Govier, J. and Davies, G. *Create your own Stage Costumes*, A. & C. Black and Heinemann, London, 1996

Hamilton Hill, M. and Bucknell, P. A. *Evolution of Fashion, Pattern and Cut from 1066 to 1930*, Reinhold, New York, NY, 1967

Hope, T. *Costumes of the Greeks and Romans*, Dover, New York, NY, 1962

Ingham, R. and Covey, L. *The Costumer's Handbook*, Prentice-Hall, Englewood Cliffs, NJ, 1980

Jans, M. *Stage Make-Up Techniques*, Van Dobbenburgh, Amsterdam and Kidderminster, 1986

Kelly, F. M. *Shakespearean Costume for Stage and Screen*, A. & C. Black, London, 1938

Kelly, F. and Schwabe, R. *Historic Costume 1490–1790*, B. T. Batsford, London, 1935

Kohler, C. *History of Costume*, Constable, London, 1963

Laver, J. *Seventeenth and Eighteenth Century Costumes*, HMSO, London, 1958

Melvill, H. *Historic Costume for the Amateur*, Rockliff, London, 1958

Motley, *Designing and Making Stage Costumes*, Studio Vista, London, 1964

Peacock, J. *Fashion Sketchbook 1920–1960*, Thames & Hudson, London, 1977

Russel, D. *Stage Costume Design*, Prentice-Hall, Englewood Cliffs, NJ, 1973

Sichel, M. *Costume Reference Series*, B. T. Batsford, London, 1977

Smith, C. Ray *Theatre Crafts Book of Costume*, Rodale Press, Emmaus, PA, 1973

Symonds, D. *Costumes of Ancient Rome*, B. T. Batsford, London, 1987

Symonds, D. *Costumes of Greece*, B. T. Batsford, London, 1987

Tilke, M. *Costume Patterns and Designs*, Zwemmer, London, 1956

Tyrrell, A. V. *Changing Trends in Fashion*, B. T. Batsford, London, 1986

Watson, P. *Costumes of Egypt*, B. T. Batsford, London, 1987

Waugh, N. *The Cut of Men's Clothes*, Faber & Faber, London, 1964

Waugh, N. *The Cut of Women's Clothes*, Faber & Faber, London, 1968

Wilcox, R. Turner *Dictionary of Costume*, Charles Scribner, New York, NY, 1969

Yarwood, D. *English Costume from the 2nd Century BC to Present Day*, B. T. Batsford, London, 1975

Zinkeisen, D. *Designing for the Stage*, The Studio, London, 1945

UK SUPPLIERS

Abracadabra
1 Bodhyfryd Road,
Llandudno LL30 2DT
(costume hire)

Angels and Bermans
119 Shaftesbury Avenue,
London WC2H 8AE *and*
40 Camden Street,
London NW1 0EN
(theatrical costume hire and
making departments)

Bazaar
5 Green Terrace,
Sunderland,
Tyne and Wear SR1 3PZ
(costumes)

Mr Benn Fancy Dress Hire
32 Saltwell View,
Gateshead,
Tyne and Wear NE8 3NT
(costume hire, make up)

Brodie
68 Drury Lane,
London WC2 5SP
(plaster, scenic paints, etc.)

Classic Costume
38 Brook Street,
Chester,
Cheshire CH1 3DZ
(period costumes)

Costume Studio Ltd.
159-161 Balls Pond Road,
London N1 4BG
(costume hire)

Fox, Charles H. Ltd.
22 Tavistock Street,
London WC2 7PY
(theatrical make up and wigs)

Freed of London Ltd.
94 St Martins Lane,
London WC2N 4AT
(ballet and dance shoes, leotards)

Hall and Dixon Ltd.
19 Garrick Street,
London WC2 9AX
(stage furnishings)

Harlequin Fancy Dress Hire
26a Brierley Lane,
Bradford,
BD4 6AA
(costumes, make up)

Joliffe, G. and Co.
48-54 Chapel Street,
Marlow,
Bucks FL7 1DD
(theatrical costumes)

Kaes, Alexis
Costume Emporium,
203 Pleasance,
Edinburgh EH8 9RU
(costumes)

Kates Costume
Unit 26,
Castlebrae Business Centre,
7 Peffer Place,
Edinburgh EH16 4BB
(costume design and making
service)

Kitbag
3b East Trinity Road,
Edinburgh EH5 3DZ
(costumes, military, historical)

Lancelyn Theatre Supplies
11 Electric Avenue,
Ferry Hinksey Road,
Oxford OX2 0BY
(sale and hire of theatrical
equipment)

Learmonth, Stuart
Unit A,
Acton Park Industrial Estate,
The Vale,
London W3 7QE
(costumes)

Leichner (London) Ltd.
436 Essex Road,
London N1 3PL
(make up)

Lewis, Bunny, Stage Door
457 Princess Road,
Manchester H20 1BH
(costume hire)

Lichfield Costume Hire
Pantomime House,
Trent Valley Road,
Nr Streethay,
Lichfield,
Staffs WS13 6EU
(designed costumes)

Masquerade
554a-556 Hagley Road,
West Quinton,
West Midlands B68 0BZ
(costume hire)

Masquerade
8 Langley Road,
Watford,
Herts WD1 3PT
(theatre dress hire)

**McMillen Stage Costume
Hire**
176 Dalry Road,
Edinburgh E11 2EG *and*
29 Waterloo Street,
Glasgow G26 B7
(musical, opera, pantomime)

Newman Hire Co.
16 The Vale,
London W3 7SB
(properties)

Old Times Furnishing
55 Chase Road,
London NW10 6LU
(furniture, properties, hire service)

US SUPPLIERS

The Pantomime Shop
Unit 2,
Heaton Street,
Mill Denton,
Manchester M34 3RG
(costume hire, theatrical supplies)

Peter Evans Studios Ltd.
11 Frederick Street,
Luton,
Beds LU2 7QW
(armour, masks, columns, plasters, etc.
also vacuum forming, rubber
mouldings, glass fibre)

Porselli
9 West Street,
London WC2H 9NE
(ballet and dance shoes, leotards)

Royal Exchange Costume Hire
692 Bolton Road,
Pendlebury,
Swinton, M27 6EL
(costume hire)

Royal Shakespeare Co. (costume
hire department)
Royal Shakespeare Theatre,
Stratford-upon-Avon,
Warks CV37 6BB
(costume hire)

Sightline, T. P. Ltd.
95 Hammersmith Grove,
London W6 0NG
(theatre period costume hire)

Theatre Stop
745 Sidcup Road,
London SE9 3SA
(costume and accessories hire)

Tiranti, Alec
70 High Street,
Theale,
Reading,
Berks RG7 5AR *and*
17 Warren Street,
London W1P 5DG
(moulding rubber, casting materials
and sculpture tools)

Broadway Costume Inc.
954 W. Washington
Chicago
IL 60607
(costumiers rental)

Brudno Art Supply Co.
601 N. State Street
Chicago
IL 60610
(brushes, artists' suppliers)

Chicago Costume Co. Inc.
1120 W. Barry
Chicago
IL 60657
(costume rental)

Fishmans Fabrics
1101 S. Des Plaines
Chicago
IL 60607
(fabrics, materials, etc.)

Kelly, Bob, Cosmetics
151 W. 46th Street
New York
NY 10036
(make up, wigs)

Nye, Ben, Inc.
5935 Bowcroft
Los Angeles
CA 90025
(make up)

Pearl Paint
308 Canal Street
New York
NY 10013
(artists' suppliers)

Showco
9029 Governor's Row
Dallas
TX 75247
(lighting, sound)

Stage-Craft Industries
5051 North Lagoon Avenue
Portland
OR 97217
(costumes, props)

Vogue Fabrics
718 732 Main
Evanstown
IL 60202
(fabrics, materials, etc.)

Please see *Yellow Pages* for further local suppliers.

INDEX